ADVANCE PRAISE

"Lalita Noronha is a rare creature, someone who feels comfortable among the conflicting demands of art and science. In the *Mustard Seed* she fulfills the promise of her earlier poems on scientific themes, ekphrastic poems on art and artists, and the post-colonial background of her family in India. In her new work, the biological sciences remain powerful sources of metaphors, especially in poems like "Specimen Child," "Apoptosis," "Passive Diffusion," and the astonishing "Beyond the Cenozoic Era." "The Python," one of the most amazing poems in this collection, beautifully demonstrates the power of biological description and begs to be compared to animalistic poems by Ted Hughes and Rainer Maria Rilke. It contains the extraordinary line "sorrow swallowed me like a python takes a rat, head first" and the section in which it's found culminates in a powerful political poem, "Bird of Paradise." Finally, something should be said about the tender love poems like "The Shirt"and the ekphrastic poem "The Widow." I have many other favorites but then this note would turn into an essay. In this sophisticated collection, enlightenment is but a page away."

— Michael Salcman, M.D., editor of *Poetry in Medicine, An Anthology of Poems About Doctors, Patients, Illness, and Healing* (Persea Books, 2015) and author of *A Prague Spring, Before & After*, winner of the 2015 Sinclair Poetry Prize from Evening Street Review.

"Whether discussing the process of passive diffusion ("moving from high to low concentration,/down its gradient,/the way honey swirls, thick in the center") or the pleasure of going to museums ("your oval gold frame,/a pendant on my heart"), Lalita Noronha writes with the precision of a trained scientist. *Mustard Seed* travels, from Goa to Baltimore, from Bethlehem to Rome, from past to present—always with a finely attended hand to guide the reader. It is a delight."

— Kim Roberts, Editor, *Beltway Poetry Quarterly*

Trixi Nordberg

MUSTARD SEED

A Collage of Science, Art and Love Poems

Lalita Noronha
Lalita Noronha

Apprentice House
Loyola University Maryland
Baltimore, Maryland

First Edition

Printed in the United States of America

Paperback ISBN: 978-1-62720-127-8
E-book ISBN: 978-1-62720-128-5

Design: Chrystelle Sharpe

Published by Apprentice House

Apprentice House
Loyola University Maryland
4501 N. Charles Street
Baltimore, MD 21210
410.617.5265 • 410.617.2198 (fax)
www.ApprenticeHouse.com
info@ApprenticeHouse.com

With my love

for Emerson
for Andrew

forever

Contents

SECTION III

SECTION IV

SECTION V

SECTION VI

I

The same lotus of our clime blooms here in the alien water with the same sweetness, under another name.

—*Rabindranath Tagore*

FORTY YEARS LATER: WHAT I KNOW

Let me say this about immigrants who burrow through the earth
to swim in rivers whose names they lisp,
Mississippi, Missouri – so many esses, hisses, misses,
the Grand Canyon they fly over with paper wings.

I love the way they step off a plane or boat into a silky twilight
towing belongings – prayer beads, bamboo flutes, jute bags –
scraps of this and that, passports and photographs,
leaving behind scorched chimneys, banana leaves,
monkeys hanging by their feet from trees.

But here is what they do not say –

We will never be whole again.
We cannot, in truth, uproot.
We will grow fins, wings, scales, tails, water-colored third eyes.
We will use our arms as legs, heels as fists, bellies and backs as floats.
We will fill our mouths with ash.

We will chill our teeth
drink the acrid wine of separation
and sleep through occasions – birth, death, days between –
for this one chance to awaken
grateful, still surprised.

BAR TALK

On bar stools,
two dirty martinis between us,
two plump, pierced olives bear witness
to ordinary words –
your family trip to some island, my kids in college,
your teaching career, my new book –
words running into piano ripples
and tinkling glasses.

I watch the bartender rim a glass in sea salt,
pour margaritas, float lime wedges on the rocks.
I can tell you still remember,
forty years later,
margaritas were my favorite drink.
Still we speak of ordinary things – anything but timing,
how fate flew you to America,
left me behind.

You drain your glass, leave the olives behind,
pay the bill, walk me to my car.
We say goodbye with barely a kiss.
But when I turn the car key,
you lean into my window, wordless,
look at me, away, and back again,
not saying what we both should say.
"Will you write about us?" you ask.

IMMIGRANT DANDELION

Deep within the mud-brown ground
of muscle and bone,
pith of water and cell,
a tap root
and a million fibrous hairs
run deep
into the belly of the earth,
find room to grow
anywhere,
between cracks in pavements,
sidewalks, walls,
among blades of pristine grass
in purest lawns.

With sunflower yellow blooms
and feathery seeds,
it dares to live and succeed
undaunted by perennial labels,
damned nuisance,
common weed.

PLANTERS AT DUSK

In rice fields, rows of inverted U-shaped shadows rise, stretch arms and straighten backs like ballerinas, twisting waists, first left, then right and left again.

Stiff from planting and patting rice saplings, the women look at the sky, now gray-blue. Chased by breeze, cotton candy clouds sweep their sari *palloos* into balloons. They turn to each other, burst into chatter, the long day's silence shattered.

Slowly, they walk to dryer land, wipe their feet, break out in twos and threes, set out for home, looking back – one long last look as shadows drown their day's work.

Still, work's not done. There's rice to boil, lentils to spice, children to bathe, men to serve, and only when the pot is scraped, each warm oblong grain eaten, dishes washed and beddings laid, will they stop and taste the starry night.

GYPSY GIRLS

They came every year, never the same ones,
never the same time of year.

Alighted upon an abandoned cricket field,
this flock of flapping geese
pitched tarpaulin tents by the light of street lamps.
Early mornings, smoke rose from piles of stones.

Children gathered sticks and twigs, older boys stole fuel –
dead branches from *peepal* trees,
dried cow dung cakes from hillsides.

Women in long multicolored skirts, bangles tinkling on arms,
gungroos on feet, brass urns on heads.

From behind a banyan tree, I untied the plantain leaf
I'd torn from clumps outside our back door.
Ate a *chapati*, slapping dough between my cheeks.

Two young girls saw me, giggled, turned, disappeared into their
tents, returned.

I stretched out my hand. They ran. I left portions on plantain
leaves, walked away.
We did this everyday. We never spoke.

Then *that* day came. It happened every year.
Uniformed police in Gandhi caps, lathis displayed.
I watched the girls flee with their families,
plantain leaves still warm in my palm.

WHAT I ASK FOR

Give me faith
the measure of one thimble and my soul will sprout,
this cracked and arid land will bloom green and gold
rich with coconut groves, paddy fields and tea plantations.

Give me faith
and I will rise like the Himalayas at dawn.

Bring me hope
in bright brass urns of monsoon rain,
between claps of thunder
under thoughts that fill ponds and swell rivers.

Bring me hope
and I will bloom like a lotus in sun.

Give me peace
which falls like sheer rain
between folds of petals, under blades of grass,
between unanswered questions, underneath the doubt,
the pain, ripe and raw,
pungent as forgiveness.

THE PRAWN WOMAN

When I open the door, she smiles as if we've met before,
a wide rimmed basket on her head.

Four hundred grams, she asks, lowering basket to floor,
she squats at the door.

I shake my head no. No. I don't want any. I don't live here.
This is where my mother lives – lived, I say in broken Hindi.

She nods. She knows. Boats just came in, she says, slipping prawns
through fingers. Pink comma-shaped rain.

One by one she peels off shells, her hands dance, bangles tinkle,
the piles grow – translucent coats, bare bodies.

One by one, she pierces the tops, pulls out black stringy guts.
Surgical precision.

Four hundred grams, she says, wrapping it up.
I reach for my wallet, separate rupees from dollars.

Nahi, nahi, not today, your mother paid me on Tuesdays.
She kept accounts, paid me half, saved the rest. For me.

Her voice is watery.
I know you, she says. Your mother always spoke of you.

You live in Umreeka. You sent us used clothes.
Your children's, Umreekan, just like new.

From a pouch she takes out a faded photograph.
See? You remember this pant?

GOA REBORN

Brown-skinned, she lies naked,
legs splayed,
awaiting conquerors and architects in polished armor.

Armies in trucks carry steel, cement, mortar,
erect hotels of grandeur with swimming pools,
marble stairs, glass elevators.

At doors and gates, men in crisp khaki uniforms
sneak peeks at alabaster women –
Russians, Germans, Americans,
who come in droves in chartered planes.

In clipped English, the men say, *Have a good day,*
not *Namaste.* They do not join their palms.

Tonight the moon draws a veil,
turns her face away from lewd displays,
and I, a foreigner too,

yearn to hear a coconut fall,
a fisherman curse,
a cock crow.

EXPLORATIONS OF A RED ANT

She stops beside my toes,
each knuckle a peak, my big red toe-nail
an unexpected foreign land.

She too has come to crossroads,
must decide which way to go,
she too has mouths to feed, a list of things to do.

She climbs, jointed antennae sensing,
hooked legs scrambling up
to where the ground is bare and brown.

She teeters at the edge,
scurries on blue highways, runs into my leg,
the steepness of Mt. Everest.

I shiver at her tickling crawl, certain I'll be bitten.
I want to flick her off, stomp her with my other foot,
but she turns and hurries down my bunion bone,

speeding home, her spirit renewed,
as if she'd always known the way,
as if she was never really lost.

FROM BOMBAY TO BALTIMORE

The Arabian Sea still flecks with fishing boats
like paper toys my father taught me to fold
and float in streams behind our home.

My plane, a silver scythe knows no ache,
splices clouds in half like cotton scarves,
shreds and tosses wispy threads afar.

Dim one-bulb huts recede, pinpoints of fire flies,
five star hotels shrink to match-box size,
coconut fronds to dainty fans.

This time, my heart, quiet and stilled,
leaves behind a billion people, maybe more,
who say their destinies are written on their foreheads.

And still I search between continents,
between sky and sky,
between then and now

for home.

THAT HALF-PAVED ROAD

I will go back to that place
where gypsies with bangles and belly rings,
jingle down a half-paved road,
pitch tents in old cricket fields,
and sing to a new moon till the police swoop down.

I will go back to that place
down a half-paved road, to the village well
where women take turns to garland brass urns,
and lower them slow, deep into that water hole,
raise them up and take them home.

I will go back to that place
where every day at noon,
a camel rider stops beside our gate.
I'll wait as the camel pushes down on plush padded toes,
and the old man pulls me up to ride that half-paved road.

I must go back to that place
for always I hear gypsies singing,
women calling, camel bells tinkling,
the monsoons crying.

II

All religions, arts and sciences are branches of the same tree.

— *Albert Einstein.*

MUSTARD SEED

for Maria; 1951-1956

I see you in kernels of rice,
palisade cells of leaves,
humble mustard seeds and redwood trees,

xylem veins carrying water, not blood,
phloem with sugars and minerals,
stomates like nostrils flaring, respiring,

transpiring, anchoring roots to earth,
branches to heaven. When you shape clouds, flood plains,
rain upon a parched palm,

you are half god, half woman,
yellow as turmeric, fragrant as cloves,
constant as the eventide.

SPECIMEN CHILD

for Anjali

*"Diatom cells are the most beautiful organisms on earth,
the most abundant species in oceans."*

— Miller and Levine

I observe you,
my little diatom

on a slide, 40x magnified,
in a buoyant drop of water,
your intricate, silicate cell walls
etched with fine lines
and brilliant glassy designs.

I watch you swim,
flicking your cilia,
lashing back at me with long flagella,
forward, sideways, diagonally,
deflecting childhood,
propelled inevitably
toward womanhood.

HOMO SAPIENS

I would molt if I could,
like reptilians, amphibians, deciduous trees,
shed my sorrow like dry skin,
this burden of *Homo sapiens,*
trapped within skeletons of bones, flesh, arteries, capillaries,
labyrinths of nerves and neurons,
organelles in cells,
cells in tissues,
tissues in organs and organ systems.

I should marvel at such intricacy, complexity.
Celebrate the human spirit,
Olympic players,
the ascent to Mount Everest.
I should applaud survivors of catastrophes –
planes, wolves, seas, disease,
the two pound baby that beats the odds and breathes –
Dolly, the cloned sheep.

Still often, the only miracle I see
lies not in chronicles of feats
but in the ache I feel
at a sparrow
shivering on an icy branch
in silvery slanted sleet.

Once Kahlil Gibran wrote, *"Yes, there is a Nirvana;*
it is in leading your sheep to a green pasture,
and in putting your child to sleep,
and in writing the last line of your poem."

A POET'S CALCULATIONS

Paired in vials of cobalt blue media,
they mate, metamorphose in ten days,
specks of eggs hatch squirming larvae,
rice-grain pupae, adult fruit flies.

My students chart sex ratios and the inheritance of traits,
black, round-bodied males, spiny oblong females,
sepia eyes, vestigial wings.
They record data, analyze, calculate gene frequencies.
It's all done in a month.

My calculations: Should I live to be, say eighty,
a respectable age in these times,
that month of teaching, a thousandth of my life-span,
flew by before I stopped to count butterflies,
or wrote the last line of this poem.

PASSIVE DIFFUSION

My students knot one end of a dialysis tube,
pour in a teaspoon of a starch and glucose solution,
tie tight the other end,
and immerse the tube in a beaker of water
spiked amber with iodine.

Slowly, the tube turns sea blue and bluer still,
as iodine diffuses *into* the tube,
turning starch dark as ink,
moving from high to low concentration,

down its gradient,
the way perfume travels from a woman's wrist
to her lover's nostrils,
or rosemary sprigs perfume the kitchen sill.

They learn that glucose diffuses *out* the tube,
sweetens water in the beaker,
moving from high to low concentration,
down its gradient,
the way honey swirls, thick in the center.

But starch, molecules too large,
are trapped within the tube,
the way grief,
blue-black blocks of sorrow
are trapped within our hearts.

I love how molecules move down gradients naturally,
with no input of energy,
the way I want my days to be,
no pumps, drips, computer chips –
just passive diffusion.

APOPTOSIS

My students laugh at the sound,
the pop, toe, the hiss,
the A in front, opposing.

I tell them it's *programmed cell death,*
but they're unimpressed.
Programmed to die? Aren't we all? Isn't that what *kismet* is?

I say, No. Not whole organisms. Not all at once.
Each cell and every cell type – skin, muscle, blood, bone
has its own clock, a predetermined life span.

Each dies quietly when the clock stops –
no spill or leak of cell contents,
no explosion, erosion, toxic emission.

And it all begins in the beginning –
taking shape in the womb,
un-webbing our webbed appendages,
spreading open our fingers and toes.

THE VISIBLE LIGHT SPECTRUM

God Himself is no rainbow.
Unseen, unfiltered, unbroken by facets of prisms,
He is the whiteness of snow, absorbing nothing,
wholly reflecting white light back to me.

Still, often I flare red anger, bruise purple, freeze blue,
sometimes, I'm the violet of violets, those shy flowers,
humble, sweet and low to the ground,
or I lie in middle wavelengths,
the yellow mint tints of autumn trees.

I want to gather these colors into which I am broken
and band them together, ember of white light,
cinder of that Great White Light
when He first created the Earth
in collisions of stars,
blaze of meteors,
bursts of fire,
blinding specks of light.

IMAGES OF HURRICANE SANDY

At first it looked like wispy white cotton

pulling tighter in whorls,
rolling on spindles, then getting looser,
five hundred – no, a thousand miles wide.

I look again: this is a monster zygote
in the ocean's womb. I watch the embryo swell,
differentiate, gestate in its amniotic sac,
kick and claw.

I watch it roar ashore –
hurl tree limbs, fences, board-walks,
toss a roller coaster into the sea,
break levies, stab cities, blacken homes, flatten hope.

I watch it rip children from their mothers' arms,
watch nurses carry new-born babies
down flights of stairs,
counting heart beats, pumping breaths.

And then, its anger spent,
it retreats, limping, gasping for breath,
back into the ocean's depths
the sounds of sorrow left behind.

AT SEA

Buoyed by memory,
we float a hundred feet beneath the sea,
arms spread wide to glide past years that
disappeared into a long good night.

Beating like soft hearts,
clouds of jelly fish rise.
Sea lions come to tickle our hands,
whiskers soft as hair.

Behind the kelp,
suspended like a question mark,
a sea horse stares
and dares us to forget.

And in this blue cosmos,
at least for one moment,
the skin of a sea-tulip blooms pink,
a hundred feet beneath the sea,

without corners
without edges
without ends

EVOLUTION IN REVERSE

I want to be
an amoeba
one-celled
fluid and shapeless
sometimes a three-pronged star,
the letter S, or M, or W
ambling along with nowhere to go
no purpose to movement,
drawn only
by changing tides and a new moon.

I want
no race or color
save what light defracts
no age, sex, sexual preference,
no political convictions
only binary fissions of nucleus and protoplasm
mitotic divisions
to infinity.

Tell me,
in all these many millions of years
what have we achieved by evolution?
Were we not immortal
long before
we knew it?

WATER HOLE

for Jon

Waitomo, says our guide, is a water hole, thirty million years old.
Limestone formed from kelp and shell was compacted,
catapulted from the sea floor.

We shout, check out the acoustics in this cavernous concert hall
where water trickles, forms crystal pillars,
stalactites, stalagmites, kiwi birds, an elephant trunk.

Further downstream, glow worms hang silken fishing lines,
trap unsuspecting midges, form a million constellations.

In the eerie glow, your little fingers point to the cave top.
We pretend it's the North Star, Big Dipper, Pollux, Castor.

The water hole, now thirty million years and one day old.

Haliotis iris: PAUA SHELL TRINKET

The size of my palm, it's an oval bowl I examine
for natural imperfections — chips, dots, unpolished spots,
remnants of marine life that hitched rides
on this bivalve's back.

Drenched in mild acid, scraped and scrubbed,
brushed with wire brushes,
the crust of marine life is ground
to dust.

Haliotis iris appears swirled in purple and blue
emerald-green ripples tint the top, crest and fall,
pearl-white pores mark breathing holes
where it's primitive heart beat.

Rebirthed and polished to a shimmer
it is folded in tissue paper and boxed,
the watery history of the Tasman Sea erased.

BEYOND THE CENOZOIC ERA

Eons from now, we'll be found,
fossils in sedimentary rock,
wrapped like Egyptian mummies in a tinge of grief.
Some higher species will think we are extinct like the dinosaurs.
Evolved pundits of paleontology
and archeology will collaborate,
carbon date our remains, sequence our DNA,
hypothesize about our species, our humanity.

But we will still be there,
in the sweetness of Nothing,
as we were before,
as we are now,
no further than is
the first crocus from spring,
the first kiss from love,
the last breath from death.

III

"Your children are not your children. They are the sons and daughters of Life's longing for itself."

– Kahlil Gibran

STARFISH ON CALVARY

for Anjali

Suspended from a nail,
a brown, spiny starfish glistens with gloss,
two arms, two legs, spread wide –
the fifth, a body and face, a Christ-man on the cross.
Tenderly, thumb and index finger trembling,
she lifts him into my outstretched palm.

"Mom, is this a real starfish?"
She is strangely calm.

Black painted buttons shine off his disk plate
on the undersurface where his mouth
once slurped up food particles
funneled in synchrony
through long, sweeping tentacles
in perfect, radial symmetry.

A tiny starfish, a baby Santa holds her hostage.
She sighs, traces outlines, in and out, five times.
How can I console my child?
"You know, echinoderms regenerate
One arm and disk grows back
into a whole new starfish!"

Underneath a miniature pine,
fat jolly guys in caps, gloves and black buttons,
consort with laughing snow girls
dressed in tantalizing white
in a red light district of Bethlehem.

She looks at her feet,
at the basket of crucified starfish
awaiting reincarnation into ornaments, magnets.
She looks in my eyes,
her face implacable, unyielding,
and then – she smiles – in compassion for me.

ALL IN THE TIMING

for Anjali

You sit cross-legged like statues of Buddha,
bodies glistening with sea water,
your upturned palms on his knees
like pink dish satellites
pick up vibrations,
the impending heart break of separation
at summer's end.

I draw my eyes away,
not daring to look,
for there I am, moons ago
walking like Jesus on water,
a teak log coarse beneath my bare feet
while he swims in the river beside me.

Your hands clasp, his fingers trace
the lines in your palms,
the veins in your wrist,
up your arm,
lingering on your ear lobe.
I will not look,
will not make unholy
your kiss.

Oh, if I could take you there,
show you that rock where I dried my hair
with his shirt
while he, like a meerkat
unfurled in the sun,
but last I heard
the river basin had dried,
the rock eroded away.

Anchored to these shores,
I watch you break free,
untethered to an umbilical cord.
We do not agree on this mystery.

You say love's sweet, never ending.
I say, it's all in the timing,
all lost in time.

VOLCANIC VALLEY

for Anjali

What lay before us was born of violence –

great rocks of molten lava, boiling mud,
black scalding water rumbled, roared,
exploded from the earth's belly,
swallowed life whole.

But now, winding our way down red clay cliffs
streaks of yellow sulfur, flecks of silica,
we pause –
beside an emerald pool, blue-green algae,
panga trees, whistling tuis, black swans.

And as mists drift apart,
in mineral waters, volcanic ash,
we find at last
fertile ground of forgiveness.

CHRISTMAS TREE

for Jon

The pine tree
that you fashioned
from a cardboard cone,
stays rooted on the mantelpiece
since you were four.

In frills of tissue needles
Monarchs dance in morning light,
at night, a silver-paper star
poised at its tip,
glitters still.

Each year the tree feels lighter,
hollowed by scrolls of years.
I hold its base,
trace your childhood
tapering to manhood.

Even now I see you standing tip toe,
your button nose
against a wintry window pane.
You want to know, you simply have to know –
who painted the pussy willow yellow.

UNWRITTEN POEM

for Emerson

That day I wanted to write you a poem,
a villanelle, ghazal, pantoum,
even just a haiku.

I wanted rippled syllables,
rhyming words to squeeze into lines
and spill over when they ought to.

But that day –
there was no language, not even alphabets
for the journey you were taking.

So, I offered you my memory
of your father's birth,
his twenty-hour journey into a world

soon to be yours.
I offered you what I couldn't
offer him that day –

my quiet aching heart yearning to take
all the sorrow you would ever face
now – now while you were still safe

before you turned the first page.

TONGARIRO

for Zarina

The Tongariro river flows above Lake Taupo, south of Hamilton,
and meets the ocean on the west coast of New Zealand.

The river flows around the curve,
Around our hearts, along the reef,
Then swerves and flows into the sea.

You went to live in *A-o-te-a-roa,*
The land of fleece and long white cloud,
Where the river flows around the curve.

Where rocks are steep, the clay too red
To drain our sorrow well before
It swerves and flows into the sea.

Where silver ferns and panga trees
Belie the anger of the sea.
The river flows around the curve,

Around our days of mud and silt,
Across the earth the river bends,
Then swerves and flows into the sea.

DOWN UNDER

for Zarina

I ask you to classify what to take:
Necessity, Luxury, Personal, Decorative, Utility —
the way my students classify Life — five kingdoms:
Monera, Protista, Fungi, Plantae, Animalia.

For New Zealand, deep in the southern hemisphere,
you wrap —
old Christmas ornaments, green-glass bowls,
photographs in two-toned frames,
our mother's dog-eared letters from India,
her chipped ceramic plate,
your first hard-earned purchase in America —
a Timex wrist watch that doesn't tick.

To each clings a story,
cloying scent of moth balls, taste of time.
We debate dates, and who said what, and where,
and who remembers being there.
We polish, embellish, hold memory to light.
The beveled mirror, re-silvered, is bubble wrapped,
encased in sheets like an Egyptian mummy,
You gaze at all you cannot take.

We pack each cardboard box,
shove something smaller into every corner,
a different shape or texture,
one into the other
so nothing stirs or breaks.

We've calculated relative costs:
crate versus cargo container, nearest ship routes.
There is no way to bring the South Pole closer, you say.
We repeat phrases —
"It's meant to be,"
"It's a good thing,"
wedging into spaces
words we cannot speak.

THE PYTHON

At eighteen, in school, when boys and girls
strolled beneath tamarind trees,
sorrow swallowed me like a python takes a rat, head first.

At noon in the zoology department,
I stood beside the python's cage,
watched his beady eyes, squashed head.

Coiled tight like a fat rope,
he lay oblivious of my eyes
counting scales, marking hues.

I waited till the keeper came,
bearing in a sack, a thrashing rat
he poured into the cage.

How it darted, climbed walls,
slipped, scurried, crouched, froze –
as the fat rope uncurled, slithered, moved.

On the floor the empty sack lay in folds,
the python undulating,
a single hump below its head.

RAW SKIN

Like yolk-less eggs
held high to a beam of light,
they have no blue, black, or sable slanted eyes,
no pencil thin or full lips,
just translucent oval faces,
navels the color of apricots,
and a plethora of breasts,
orange halves, grapefruit, cantaloupe.

Silver-tasseled thread, fuchsia beads
dangle on pink nipple pegs.
Bare buttocks like alabaster saucers
or burnished copper plates rotate,
hips undulate.
Ankles on glittering stilts,
appear, disappear, reappear.
Raw skin floats.

On the iridescent slinky stage,
childhoods weighted with green bills
in garter belts and G-strings splash –
sting of metal on water,
sink in wells of sorrow,
leaving ripples,
wedge of light glinting.

BIRD OF PARADISE

Cradled in leaves, two-feet long,
sword-shaped and edged in crimson,
the yolk-yellow bird of paradise nestles
as bees hover about and settle.

Curled up on a wide marble ledge,
dragon flies sail above my head,
I move with the sun, unfurl behind pillars
for shade and open the newspapers—

A saffron-robed priest awakens from his meditation,
a knife gleaming at his throat.

A man's yamulka is yanked off his head,
tossed like a baseball cap.

A dove-like nun's bland brown eyes bleed
while they splay and pluck her feathers.

A doe-eyed girl climbs from the window of her burkha,
meets her husband-hunter's eyes.

I turn to the bird of paradise—

A bloom with five petals, one boat shaped,
four little men rowing at the hull,
thirteen heads bobbing.

Each shoot bears sprays of three or four blooms,
all asymmetrical and exquisite,
all hand designed by the same artist
we call by different names—

Jesus, Allah, Vishnu, Buddha —
even as we kill, defile, and make the daily headlines.

MILITARY TREES

It depends on the orders they receive.

Sometimes they are called to be tornadoes,
EF-5 at least, hard as teak,
volleys of bullets ricochet off their bark.

Sometimes they are thunderstorms, hurricanes, cyclones,
sometimes a patrolling summer breeze, olive trees.
Still, what solace is there in stripping them clean?

Who does not long for simple pleasures – perhaps gardening?
How long till fathers see their babies, till mothers read them stories?
How long must children kiss computer screens?

IV

"Here we are, trapped in the amber of the moment. There is no why."

— *Kurt Vonnegut.*

THE FACE

In the center of your chin
soft brown hair curves up and stops,
touches your lower lip,
a wide W with rounded bottoms.

It defines your jaw and especially your lips with darker furrows,
and from the tip of your nose,
your face opens wide
like a desert, parched and arid,

and just when I fear there is no oasis,
I fall into two
dark
wells,
where I stop to drink.

THE SHIRT

The collar is limp, the points
rounded from washing and ironing,
the sleeves are shorter,
the girth narrower
wrung dry after twenty eight years.

Interlinking, midnight blue and crimson
diamonds stretch point to point,
centers like dark pupils, dilating,
gazing in my direction.
You wore it open at the collar with blue jeans.

You had it on the night we met.

THROUGH BINOCULARS: WHAT I SEE FROM MY THIRD FLOOR BALCONY.

High in trees, plump magnolia blooms
frame my periscope, each bloom a fractal,
yellow dipped in orange, chalice like.

Trees, branches, leaves, once so far away, are right here,
so near, I could touch them.

Sky, an expanse of blue, so wide, it might be the sea,
were it not for lean branches criss-crossing my lens.

I think of you, out of my field of vision,
out of reach, a patch of isolated blue.
Sea or sky, who can tell?

WHAT WE CANNOT NAME

At the aquarium,
we watch the dolphin show,
the way the babies learn to trust,
imitate, flip, belly flop, drop deep into the pool,
the way they synchronize their days,
in ways we never could.

Sea horses cling to leaves,
butter-nut yellows, oak-nut browns.
Sea rays glide beside black shadows,
spotted, dotted with patches,
a hammerhead shark.
A silver white curls around a leaf.

In the rain forest,
purple finches flit and flirt, red-winged blackbirds
perch and sing, wings spread wide,
a scarlet tanager catches our eyes,
the way light catches darkness and swings
it around, a tourniquet of guilt for what we cannot name,

as the sun slides his tongue
under dry tattered leaves.

HOW WINTER CLINGS

Dressed in green,
brown branched arms
wave aside the chill,
kiss summer's lips,
flaunt sunlit limbs,
sprout buds, blossoms, seeds.

But look again –
how winter clings,
dried discarded leaves,
some severed branches,
a skinless trunk,
a wingless bird,
a broken nest.

PHONY LINES

It's in your breath, strung along the phone lines, a little drawn out,
warmer. Sometimes, a sudden laugh at strange words I still use –
the *boot* of my car, *serviettes* I'll restock,
masala kheema and *ek dozen unda.*

I wait for a teasing line, a quick,
funny retort, the start of back and forth repartee.
I forget that we're winding down the clock, burning down the house.
It shouldn't take so long.

You suck in your breath, squeeze your heart,
stuff the words you might have said back into your mouth.
"Take care; I'll talk to you soon," you say,
your voice a million miles beyond the moon.

IN SPACE

If I step lightly on water like Christ,
tread waves till I touch the horizon,
lift and soar to outer space
as Saturn's tenth ring, or
Pluto's first moon;
if I lie beside the Virgin,
below the Lion's tail,
one hundred and ninety light years away,
could I escape those cold, blue,
elliptical moons in your eyes?

THIRTY-TWO YEARS

Throat dry, I crave
half-forgotten moments,
that glass of iced water,
wedge of lemon floating,
a bowl of barley soup,
that cup of mint tea,
you brought me
every now and then.

But always,
always at dawn,
I wait for those two cups of coffee,
hot and sweet,
we sipped together,
year after year,
just short of twelve thousand cups
in all.

JOURNAL ENTRIES

As I riffle through the years,
a journal of my marriage,
I stop –
re-read lines, try to decipher clues,
skip forward and back,
looking for an arc of suspense,
a premonition,
a foreshadowing, a plot.

I check entry dates –

1979: that night in the dark delivery room
the silhouette of your face etched
in the space between the pain.
1999: your business sold,
those dark nights you'd take the dog out,
lean against my car, smoke a cigar,
the silhouette of your face barely visible.

2001: the house sold,
four bedrooms, sunroom, a fireplace,
some disrepair, but it passed inspection,
the silhouette of your face as you handed over keys.

I thumb thirty-two yellowed pages,
blurred, dog-eared,
water-stained, crossed out words,
searching for the mystery,
the heart of the story.
It must be somewhere,
hidden among these blank pages
at the end.

TASTING TIME

I nibble at minutes
one peanut at a time,
each second,
a grain of rice,
one raisin.
I taste each moment without you,
the form,
smooth oblong nut,
ellipsoid rice,
the wrinkled skin of the raisin
rough on the roof of my mouth.

V

"*Painting is poetry which can be seen and not heard, and poetry is a painting which is heard and not seen.*

– Leonardo da Vinci

SISTERHOOD

After "Woman in Profile" by Thomas Couture, 1815-1879;
Baltimore Museum of Art.

I want to touch you, not as men would,
not your white breast,
upturned nipple, trembling,
not the swan-like arc of your neck,
wing of collarbone,
lobe of your ear, unadorned.

I want to cup your face, turn
your head, raise your downcast
eyes, unbraid your hair,
cascade it
over your bared breast,
button your gown.

I want to wear you
in your oval gold frame,
a pendant on my heart,
as many million women would,
who, like you,
have turned away.

WOMAN OF THE MANGO

After Paul Gauguin's Vahine no te vi, Woman of the Mango;
Baltimore Museum of Art

Tehemana, you may be his Tahitian Eve,
his thirteen-year-old model, his wife,
still, you are not his only island girl.

Told to pose with a mango,
you arrange your hair in waterfalls of onyx,
except for a single ringlet you bring forward.

You select your plum-purple dress,
the one that falls in folds
in front, apron-like.

Orange-red, tip still green,
the mango fills your right palm,
its weight upon your wrist.

Then, you turn away,
tuck your copper-warm chin
into your shoulder.

You hold within your naked soul
what he hasn't yet been told,
the fruit you alone must bear.

THE KISS

After Auguste Rodin's The Kiss; Baltimore Museum of Art

It's the way your hand rests
on her thigh,
barely touches
her buttock,
your thumb poised above,
the way she sits
sideways astride between
your legs opened wide.

It's the way her arm encircles
your neck,
one on your breast,
the way she lifts
her face
from the cave of your arm,
the way you take
her only with your lips.

It's how we know
what drove Adam and Eve from
Paradise,
why Paolo and Francesca left
The Gates of Hell,
why we stand
and gaze,
and gaze.

THE WIDOW

After George Wesley Bellows' The Widow; Baltimore Museum of Art

Now that the mourners have left and the house is still,
I imagine you will push back your wicker chair,
pick up the vase of scarlet blooms
and walk into the bedroom, now only yours.

You'll put down your black-bordered handkerchief,
unclasp your coal-black cloak,
disrobe, unknot your hair,

perhaps you'll look in the mirror,
see a furrowed river delta, silt cheeks,
daybreak-blue eyes, untouched by bitter burning suns,

perhaps too, you'll see a flower face,
rose-bud mouth, a cinched waist,
a girl in taffeta and tulle,

your hands, veined and parchment thin,
will bloom pink,
your ring, yellow gold.

But until you're ready to rise,
to extinguish the lamp and lay away this day,
I, too, will sit here in silence with you.

ILLUSION

After Jan Van Goyen's View of Rhenen, 1656; Baltimore Museum of Art

This is what I see:
sleepy clouds along the inlet,
pinpricks of light in windows,
church spires on distant hills.

But for salmon sunlit patches, it is dark.
But for paddles slapping ripples,
it is still.

On the river bank,
cows chew their cuds,
men bend over fishing nets,
bring in the evening catch,
seagulls hover.

In the brooding twilight,
I am swept back forty years,
to the Ganges river bank,
to temples and clay lamps,
saris washed and drying,
waist-deep in water, women praying

Until, two windmills far on a hill
pull me back to another land,
another's home,
which for an instant was my own.

BETRAYAL

After Thomas Cromwell Self Portrait c. 1890; Baltimore Museum of Art

Too young to be so stark,
your eyes accuse me as if it was I,
not she, who betrayed you.

I imagine she traced your bristled jaw,
your thinned mustache,
her finger tips over your open lips.

I come close, tilt my head,
reverse my steps, swerve aside,
yet your lucent eyes follow me.

I imagine what I cannot see,
what she left behind,
fiery loins, a lean quiet man.

Do you dare me to touch you,
tip your silly bowler hat,
unlock you?

THE PIETA

After Michelangelo Buonarroti, Vatican City, Rome

O lady, you part your legs,
not to birth the one you grew within your womb,
but to cradle a man –
his buttocks in the hammock of your gown,
your elbow an arc for his shoulders,
stilled temples on your breast.

You gaze at purpled gashes, blood reds, pinks,
his body still warm,
your boy crowned king.

For this alone were you born.
For this alone was he born.
O Mary,
look up from his face.
Tell me,
For what was I born?

DEFIANCE

After "Young Girl on a Chair" by Giacomo Manzu,
Bronze Sculpture, 1955, Baltimore Museum of Art Garden

Your tiny tight buttocks clench the wicker seat,
bronze legs and thighs,
straight as stilts
root your soles
to earth.

Your belly glistens below budding breasts,
at your waist, bent elbows rest,
your arms are stretched,
fingers interlaced in prayer
cover that sacred place.

But it's all there
in your face, insolent pout,
steeled eyes averted,
nappy hair pulled straight back
in a perky pony tail.

It's clear you will not confess,
not repent,
content to do time,
and do it all
again.

ENVY

After Jose Ruiz De Rivera's Stainless steel with internal motor
Baltimore Museum of Art

Mounted six feet high on a black marble base,
the stainless steel ballerina
curves her mirrored tapered arms to the sky,
and turns –
slow, imperceptible turns,
reflecting veins on leaves,
skin on trees, scraps of cloud,
sprints of air, glints of sun –
her vision ever-changing,
expanding and condensing,
sliding, sweeping, vanishing,
as she turns –
a carousel of uncertainty,
embracing the world,
while I stand here tethered at the base,
seeing only my face mirrored in black marble,
eclipsed.

THE PLATTER

After Niagara Falls, from the American Side.
Potter: Enoch Wood and Sons, Baltimore Museum of Art

Birthed on your potter's wheel
and fired in a kiln,
I imagine this platter
on my Thanksgiving table,
a large cobalt-blue oval dish; the rim,
the river, horse shoe crabs and heart-shaped cockles,
channeled whelks and periwinkles swimming off
the edge, their light and dark blue
markings toppling onto my damask
table cloth. And in the center, swirled in light
and shade and sheen, white waterfalls cascade,
foam-filled clouds and skies dissolve,
smudged trees like sentries, watch.

I stop at your inscription:
After Niagara Falls, from the American Side;
as if it matters which side,
whose splendor,
as if we, like the trees,
can't watch waterfalls fall,
and quietly give thanks.

COFFEE URN

English (1800-1825)
After Samuel Roberts and George Cadman, Sheffield.
Baltimore Museum of Art

It might have been a Vatican chalice,
consecration vessel for water and wine
at St. Peter's Cathedral in Rome,
home to cardinals and popes—
but for that ornate spout jutting out—
an afterthought when you changed your mind.

A silver-and-wood body of beauty,
voluptuous and shimmering,
pineapple crowns fit for a king
mounted on a triangular pedestal,
destined for his buffet table,

but for two question-mark handles
staring at each other—
asking, what?
All this for coffee?
Not wine?

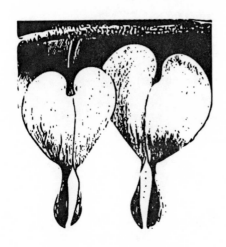

VI

"I cannot keep your waves," says the bank to the river. "Let me keep your footprints in my heart."

— *Rabindranath Tagore*

I WAS THERE

She had never looked more beautiful
than on her wedding day,
I know,
I was there
in the dew of her rose bouquet.

The night I was born,
she wore purple on her skin,
a red slit below her naval,
black moons beneath her eyes.

Angels came to claim her,
I know,
I was there
holding her down,
tethering her to earth with my umbilical cord.

MIRROR IMAGE

Sitting inside myself,
I watch how my hair speckles,
eyes fringed thin
like autumn trees,
this face an abandoned tributary,
silt the Ganges left behind.

On my feet,
my mother's bunions, jagged rocks.
On my hands,
her skin stretched taut and thin
slices apricots, dices mangoes
strip by strip.

How our fingers grip
fruit that must die.

MOTHER'S BUNIONS

Each year, your bunions kept encroaching,
jutting out like boulders over a ledge,
brazen, unapologetic, skewing your helpless toes
that lay upon each other,
onion-skin thin over bone.

When asked what you'd like from America,
your answer was always the same –
"shoes, wide and soft, toes closed,
so I can walk to church.
These hard, paved roads hurt."

Armed with tracings of your feet
I'd trudge through shoe stores,
measure and match up drawings to the widest, round-toed flats,
and ask the attendant to stretch them some more.
In disbelief he'd shake his head.

On my last visit, you lay on your back,
legs bowed, heels on sheet,
big knobbed bunions protruding,
toes tilted, slanting.
I did not bring you shoes.

These days my feet throb
as if your bones still live in me,
as if my toes have learned the ways of yours,
as yours did from your mother's feet before,
as if there is no other way to be.

MOTHER'S PASSPORT

On the tarmac to a plane, now three hours late,
my mother walks,
her feet laced in bunion guards,
heel cups and corn removers.

In her suitcase,
instant soups, extra sharp cheese,
Efferdent tablets she'll break in half to make last.
A pair of shoes she'll never use.

She has shown her passport,
midnight teal, Ashoka lion seal,
The Republic of India embossed in gold,
it's getting old, soon to expire, she's told.

She nods,
yes she knows,
she knows,
turns and waves goodbye.

JUST FINE

"Only beer," my mother says,
"Not as bad as it used to be. He drinks beer,
and sometimes Pepsi spiked with whiskey. And
please don't you use that AA word
 Not in this house.
By the sea at Mount Mary's colony, there's an ashram for *real*
drunks with no decent jobs.
He is not like *that!*
Imagine, he won Best Employee
of his company two years in a row."

Her words float on curling smoke,
"Your brother is fine,

                    just fine,

                              fine."

MIRACLE AT CANA

I watch my mother's face,
the way a film falls over her eyes,
the way she sets her mouth
and drops the subject.
Like the sparrow that lives in the hemlock tree,
small, brown, busy twittering, nesting,
she searches for the meaning,
waiting for his return to sobriety,
waiting for a miracle,
for Lazarus to rise,
for the wine
to change back to water.

RITUAL

Mother turns the door knob,
enters your room,
a glass of iced water in one hand,
a plate of warm food in the other.

Slumped again in your easy chair,
you sing the same song,
a slow, slouching, tuneless dirge
like bullocks ambling on unpaved roads

stopping suddenly, mid-note,
till a whip cracks and
sends them clanging forth.
"Hush," Mother whispers,

"Shh! The neighbors will hear."
She puts aside the whiskey bottle,
turns the TV up loud,
pulls down window shades,

and draws her shawl tight
around her breasts,
as if her heart has
ears.

SPONGE BATH

Two hours late this morning,
the aide is here at last to
turn her on her side,
face to the wall,
raise her arms, splay her legs.
In the doorway out of sight,
I see my mother cling to the headboard,
her hair a silver fluff
of dandelion, her buttocks flat as dinner plates,
her skin phyllo-thin.

I watch how the aide chucks my mother's chin,
scrubs her neck, rubs behind her ears,
picks up her fallen breasts,
lifts her legs, scours between,
thuds them down.

Hey, I want to shout, slow down, not so rough,
but dare I disrupt, dare I find another caretaker?
I – who did not stay,
and won't for much longer –
have no say in such matters.

Please, I want to beg, please,
I'll pay you more – in dollars –
in advance, a secret between us.

ACROSS BONES

We lie still
in the void
between then and now,
my grandmother, mother and I,
like bound pages in a book,
back to front,
arms about waists
tucked in decades,
one hundred years, or more.

But when, on moonless nights,
I start to cry,
my grandmother reaches far
across my mother's bones,
gathers my tears.
"It's all right; it will pass," she says,
"these things happen,
have happened before,
and will again."

I inhale her breath,
and her mother's mother's breath,
vapors of ten thousand years,
and years before that.
When today becomes yesterday,
and days before that,
she knows I will stretch across
my daughter's bones,
touch my granddaughter's cheek,
say what she has said.

We lie still
in the space
as one by one
my grandmother puts back my tears
into my eyes.

MOTHER'S STORIES

The monsoons cried for days when
as a child you told me stories,
family histories of who was who,
and how they came and went,
and whose ancestral flesh
we wear.

The boy,
a priest, your cousin,
who fell in love and lost his girl,
his mind, his faith, too,
who spent his days wandering streets in search
of what he never knew.

The woman,
his mother, who lost her way one moonless night
and stepped into an open well without a sound,
found when that fiery ball
shone upon her,
afloat.

The little girl,
your aunt, who played upon a pile of wood,
and bitten by a snake, fell asleep,
the wood your father's father used
to go ahead and build the house he meant to build,
his child's face on every wall.

You have told me stories,
round and round in rings of years
your words have taken root,
bloomed into a story tree
which I now must tell,
now that I've been called to speak

your name.

CORONATION

They intone the last rites,
sprinkle holy water,
close the lid over your eyes,
burn incense, whisper.
When the organ plays,
the palanquin is lowered.

Hands pour blossoms,
rose and marigold,
against the wind petals flutter, fold.
When my turn comes, I toss a handful,
pouring my childhood,
emptying our splintered years.

This day is auspicious Mother,
your crucifixion, my coronation,
you, the last of your generation,
I, the first in mine.
Listen to their swelling voices,
Listen how they call my name.

THE WIND SPEAKS

That night
the wind flew in,
whistling where have you been?
I've been looking for you
under the sycamore trees in the cemetery.

He cried out your name,
touched the places you'd lived –
your bed, night stand,
the kitchen window.
And then he left.

The window curtain stilled.
I was lying in your bed.
The sheets smelled fresh,
no scent of tiger balm, eucalyptus, old limbs,
just me within your imprint.

I lay still.
A silver crescent hung in the sky.
My right hand held your rosary,
my left hand held yours –
white light.

And the wind returned,
a breeze now,
as if to keep us company,
as if he knew you were still here,
as if he knew you wouldn't leave.

WING

When I am asleep
I find a moon rock
and with it, sometimes
an angel and a purple finch

a crawling crab
a cawing crow
the angel with one wing

when I am asleep
craters fill with boiling mud
these are merely meanderings

these avian, human, crustacean
creatures of air, land and water
of fairies and sorcerers

when I am asleep
the moon rock is my bed
for me there is no other way

no way to know if I am today
or was before the dinosaurs

sometimes the wingless angel crawls

Acknowledgments

Crab Orchard Review, "**Mirror Image**"

A Thousand Worlds, An Anthology of Indian Women Writers, (Aurat Books, ed. Husta and Nellore) "**Coronation**"

Science Poetry Anthology, (Anamnesis Press, ed. Keith Daniels) "**Beyond the Cenozoic Era**" "**In Space**"

A Contemporary Anthology of Asian American Women's Poetry (Deep Bowl Press, ed. Anne Marie Fowler) "**Mustard Seed**" "**Journal Entries**" "**Raw Skin**"

JMWW, http://jmww.150m.com/Noronha.html; "**At Sea**"

New Lines from the Old Line State, An Anthology of Maryland Writers, (MWA Book, ed. Allyson E. Peltier) "**Thirty-two Years**" "**Waning Moon**"

Thanal online, "**I was There**" "**Half an Earth Away**"

Little Patuxent Review, "**Across Bones**" "**The Visible Light Spectrum**"

The Orange Room, http://www.theorangeroomreview.webs.com; "**Mother's Bunions**"

Spillway, "**Mother's Stories**"

Pirene's Fountain, "**From Bombay to Baltimore**" "**Phony Lines**"

Poetry Anthology: Life in me like grass on fire: love poems (MWA Book, ed. Laura Shovan) "**Tasting Time**" "**Specimen Child**" "**Mother's Passport**"

Arlington Literary Journal "**Bar Talk**"

WordWrights, "**Ritual**"

Function at the Junction, "**All in the Timing**" "**Homo sapiens**"

The Baltimore Sun, "**Starfish on Calvary**"

Fodderwing, "**The Shirt**"

The Light Ekphrastic, "**Defiance**"

The Pedestal Magazine, "**But for That**"

http://www.thepedestalmagazine.com/Secure/Content/ cb.asp?cbid=5300

Thy Mother's Glass: Poems for Mothers and Daughters, (A WordHouse Book, Baltimore Writers' Alliance, ed. Diane Scharper) "**Christmas Tree**"

Beltway Poetry Quarterly, "**Sisterhood**" "**Gypsy Girls**" "**Prawn Woman**"

Serenity Prayers: Prayers, Poems, and Prose to Soothe Your Soul. (ed. June Cotner, Andrews McNeel Press) "**Forgiveness**"

Get Well Wishes: Prayers, Poems, Blessings: (ed. June Cotner, Harper Collins) **"Hope"**

Suvarnarekha: An Anthology of Indian Women Poets Writing in English, The Poetry Society of India. (ed. Nandini Sahu) **"Beyond the Cenezoic Era" "From Bombay to Baltimore"**

The Dance of the Peacock: An Anthology of English Poetry from India (Hidden Brook Press, Ed. Vivekanand Jha) ***"Evolution in Reverse" "Immigrant Dandelion" "Sponge Bath"***

Mascara Literary Review: ***"The Python," "Waimangu Valley," "Butterfly"***

A selection of these poems also appear in my chapbook, *Her Skin Phyllo-thin (Finishing Line Press)*

About the Author

Born in India, Lalita Noronha came to the US on a Fulbright travel grant and earned her Ph.D. in Microbiology/Biochemistry from St. Louis University School of Medicine. She is a widely published research scientist, poet, and writer. As a scientist, she has worked at the National Institute of Health, in the biopharmaceutical industry, and as a teacher/department chair at St. Paul's School for Girls. She has published over 100 science papers and abstracts.

Her literary work has appeared in many literary journals and anthologies in India, Australia, Canada, New Zealand and the US including *The Baltimore Sun, The Christian Science Monitor, Catholic Digest, Crab Orchard Review, The Cortland Review*, and *Gargoyle* among others. She is the author of a short story collection, *Where Monsoons Cry* (BlackWords Press) which won the Maryland Literary Arts Award and a poetry chapbook, *Her Skin Phyllo-thin* (Finishing Line Press.)

Others credits include a Maryland Individual Artist Award in fiction, awards from *Arlington Literary Journal*, Dorothy Daniels National League of American Pen Women, and Pushcart nominations in Poetry and Creative Nonfiction. Former President of the Maryland Writers' Association, she is an editor for the *Baltimore Review*, and a guest editor for the science-themed issue of *Little Patuxent Review*. She has also been featured several times on WYPR's The Signal. Her website/blog is www.lalitanoronha.com.

Apprentice House is the country's only campus-based, student-staffed book publishing company. Directed by professors and industry professionals, it is a nonprofit activity of the Communication Department at Loyola University Maryland.

Using state-of-the-art technology and an experiential learning model of education, Apprentice House publishes books in untraditional ways. This dual responsibility as publishers and educators creates an unprecedented collaborative environment among faculty and students, while teaching tomorrow's editors, designers, and marketers.

Outside of class, progress on book projects is carried forth by the AH Book Publishing Club, a co-curricular campus organization supported by Loyola University Maryland's Office of Student Activities.

Eclectic and provocative, Apprentice House titles intend to entertain as well as spark dialogue on a variety of topics. Financial contributions to sustain the press's work are welcomed. Contributions are tax deductible to the fullest extent allowed by the IRS.

To learn more about Apprentice House books or to obtain submission guidelines, please visit www.apprenticehouse.com.

Apprentice House
Communication Department
Loyola University Maryland
4501 N. Charles Street
Baltimore, MD 21210
Ph: 410-617-5265 • Fax: 410-617-2198
info@apprenticehouse.com • www.apprenticehouse.com

CPSIA information can be obtained
at www.ICGtesting.com
Printed in the USA
FFOW03n0130191217
44076613-43344FF